The Prison on the Moor

The astonishing story of Dartmoor Prison
by Robert Sanderson

The old War Prison

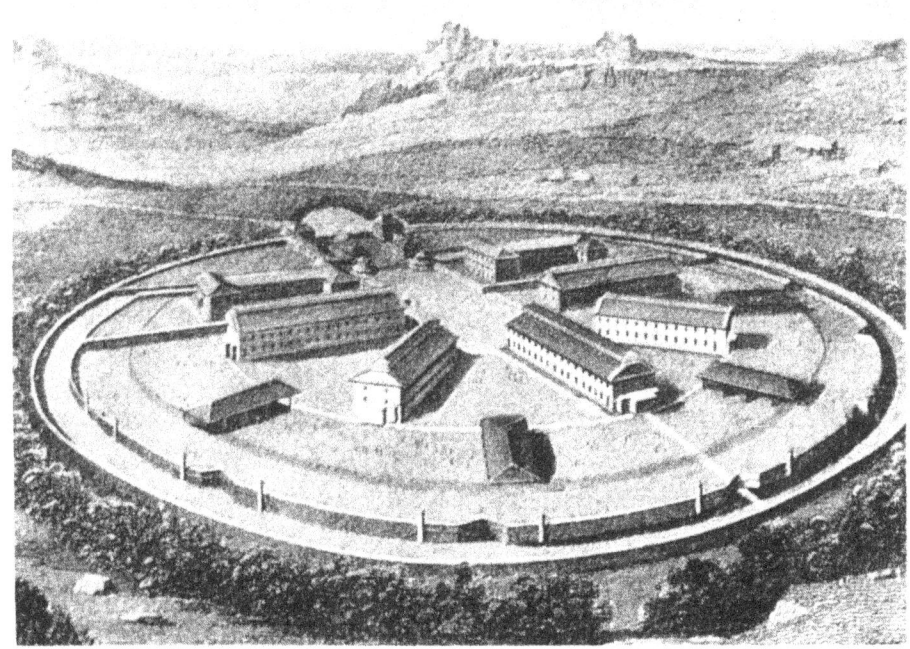

This version of the book is virtually as originally published, presenting the work of Robert Sanderson. There are now additional pages at the back providing information about the publisher, Arthur L Clamp.

The republishing project is being managed by Arthur's grandson, Steven Gibson. We aim to find all the research that he was involved in publishing, preserving it for the next generation as part of 'The Clamp Collection'.

Introduction

THOUSANDS of visitors come to Dartmoor each year to see its rugged hills and tors, to enjoy for a few hours or days the quietness of its landscape and to take at least one brief look at the granite prison which many have read about and only a few have actually seen.

Some are disappointed at what they see, others take a rather curious look at its gaunt buildings and then go on without ever giving it any further thought. Some, however, stay for awhile and try to picture some of the events that have hit the national newspaper headlines about life in the prison and the attempts at escape from this often mist-enshrouded area.

Like many things that hit the headlines there is often more than an element of exaggeration in the story and so often the truth is much plainer than one is led to believe. This is certainly true of Dartmoor prison. The day-to-day events take place with almost regular monotony and the local people go about their tasks without giving a lot of thought to this prison which chills the heart of those associated with the underground world of the major cities of the country.

But what is the story of this granite building that holds many criminals sentenced for their notorious acts? Well, it's a story with a fascinating history in which men of many nationalities and colour have been kept, men caught up in wars between England and France on the one hand, and England and America on the other hand. It's a story of hardships, crowded rooms and of many attempts at getting off the moor, some being successful, over the 170 or so years of its life. It also includes a period of time when the old buildings were left empty and ruinous, a time when it was going to be used for housing orphans from London.

Situated in the heart of Dartmoor has brought its own problems in running the prison, apart from the advantages it gives in helping to prevent escapes. Severe winters have cut off Princetown for many days and reduced food stocks to a very low level, water supplies often froze and temperatures frequently fell well below freezing point which considerably increased hardship in the old unheated prison.

It is very difficult nowadays to visualize the conditions under which men were kept in the old buildings especially with overcrowding and outbreaks of disease. The division of the prisoners of war into social classes and the way they organised themselves and their style of living, will come as an additional surprise to the enquiring visitor to Dartmoor.

However, there have been many alterations in the prison. The organisation, routine of work and number of inmates bear no resemblance to the years when it housed war prisoners. There are now good workshop facilities for training men for various trades, up-to-date medical resources and many opportunities for recreational activities. Study classes, games and physical training are also available to inmates who wish to use them.

It is hoped that this illustrated booklet will help in telling most of the interesting story of this famous prison to the enquiring visitor.

I wish to express my appreciation to the Governor, Deputy Governor and Staff for their help in supplying information and for being taken around the prison and also for supplying and allowing to be reproduced the various photographs. Assistance and advice was given by library Staffs at Plymouth and Exeter for which I am indebted.

Some of the photographs are crown copyright and are reproduced with the permission of HM Stationery Office.

Princetown

THE village was named in honour of the Prince of Wales, afterwards King George IV, and claims to be one of the highest in England standing 1,430 feet above sea level.

It grew and developed as the prison became larger after 1806, although there were a few buildings here before this date, the principal one being the Plume of Feathers, which largely served the needs of the tin miners and hill farmers roundabout.

This part of the moor was developed by Sir Thomas Tyrwhitt, Lord Warden of the Stannaries, who also promoted the Princetown to Tavistock road and the construction of the old Dartmoor railway.

Princetown almost lies in the centre of the Dartmoor National Park close to the junction of the main roads crossing the moor. The siting of the prison here was suggested by Sir Thomas Tyrwhitt as part of his plan to open up the barren hills. The fact that this is one of the wettest and foggiest areas around may have also been a factor in its favour. The earlier difficulties in reaching this spot can now hardly be appreciated with the good roads over the moor and, of course, travelling by car and not on foot.

Visitors often use Princetown as a focal point for exploring the moor. The prison can be seen from where the Devonport leat under passes the road to Two Bridges. Part of the prison farm area can also be seen as well. The leat was cut to supply the needs of Devonport Dockyard and ships coming in for restocking.

An enjoyable hour or more can be spent in this locality going to the church and seeing the various memorials and the unmarked graves of convicts. North Hessary tor pylon, used for beaming television programmes over a large area, stands high above Princetown, its head often in the clouds. Below the village, on the south side, is Tor Royal which was built as early as 1798 by Sir Thomas Tyrwhitt as part of an estate. Cars can be taken down as far as Whiteworks.

Finally Princetown is seldom without a few Dartmoor ponies wandering about its square but they must not be fed.

The War Prison 1809 to 1816

THE prison was built as a direct result of the war between England and France which was renewed in 1803. The two existing prisons in the country and six prison hulks lying at Plymouth soon became overcrowded with French prisoners so it was decided to build a larger prison at Princetown, the foundation stone of which was laid on 20th March, 1806, by the Lord Warden of the Stannaries, Sir Thomas Tyrwhitt.

The first draft of prisoners was marched up from Plymouth in 1809 and by the end of the year there were some 5,000 men housed in five buildings within two high boundary walls. The staff comprised of thirty-three under a Captain Cotgrave and garrison battalion of 500 men from the Militia. These were increased to 1,200 when more prisoners brought the total to around 9,000 in 1812 which eventually included American prisoners of war.

In spite of the crowded conditions and scant accommodation, the French soon settled down to their new way of life more or less grouping themselves according to rank, wealth and class. The first class was known as *Les Lordes* being men of good family who lived in a separate building within the walls known as *Petit cautionnemont*. They were officers drawing money from their bankers via agents in London who patronised the daily market and paid other prisoners to act as servants. They led a life of ease swaggering about in clothing made by other prisoners and engaging in duelling, gambling, holding theatricals and other similar pursuits.

The next were composed of *Les Labourers*, who having no money to draw on, were obliged to work as tailors, jewellers, model-makers, schoolmasters, forgers, carvers of bone and wood and many other activities through which they were able to earn money. These were the thrifty prisoners. *Les Indifferents* made up the third group who did nothing but laze about the prison and simply existed on the very scant official rations.

The last group called themselves *Les Romains* who were confined to the upper floors of each building, known as the cock-lofts. They had resorted to gambling and turned their clothing, bedding and even rations into money only to eventually lose it. They lived almost like animals, naked and covered with vermin and getting what they could from the garbage heaps for food. The conditions in which they lived were appalling being overcrowded, noisy and with fighting taking place as a normal daily event. In 1812

French Prisoners of War

This old photograph shows one of the buildings which housed French prisoners of war.

they were completely separated from the other prisoners and an inner wall built to stop them annoying staff and inmates. An inquiry was held into their way of living which resulted in 436 men being transferred to the prison hulks at Plymouth until the end of the war.

By 1812 there were seven prison buildings within the walls, an infirmary and petty officers' prison. The buildings were 60 feet long, three-storeyed and paved with concrete. A large flight of granite steps connected each of the floors. The windows simply consisted of square holes, two feet wide, heavily barred and without glass. There was no heating of any kind apart from a few small stoves bought by the prisoners themselves. 500 men were confined to each floor, so each building held about 1,500 persons. The noise and heat of the men must have been overpowering and soon resulted in many outbreaks of disease including gaol fever, better known as typhus. In November 1809 an epidemic of measles swept through the prison and some 500 died over a period of three months out of 5,000 prisoners. Time and time again minor outbreaks of disease occurred through the unsavoury conditions and lack of simple hygiene.

When one views the prison today, it is almost impossible to picture the crowds of men, dressed in a variety of tattered, yet colourful, uniforms wandering around and speaking in a foreign tongue. What with the

Punishments

English troops guarding the French and American soldiers and people coming up to the daily market to buy or sell goods, this must surely have been one of the most cosmopolitan scenes in Devon.

The only punishments which seem to have been meted out was to reduce the already scanty rations to two-thirds and confine very troublesome prisoners in the cachot. This was a tiny building of rough masonry measuring 20 feet square with two openings under the eaves 6 inches by 4 inches. The door was iron-plated on both sides and a 8 inch square hole allowed food to be passed through. There was no furniture or even straw to sleep upon, just the stone floor.

The Market

Men were kept in here for upwards of six months without light or being allowed out for exercise. Such was one style of punishment which happily is no longer with us.

A surprising feature of the early prison was the daily market allowed within the walls to which tradesmen, farmers and pedlars from Plymouth would bring in goods for sale to the better off prisoners. The agent fixed the price of goods according to those prevailing at Tavistock and before very long a considerable trade developed benefiting the area for many miles around. Goods made by the prisoners were also sold or exchanged and there eventually sprang up a friendship between the country people and the higher-class prisoner. A wide variety of produce was brought in and a surprising variety of goods were made, often very skilfully, by the prisoners to enhance their living conditions.

Moving about the prison and even going out of the main buildings seems to have been quite a common practice, at least with the French officer class. Some were out on parole living in Devon and obtaining money from their bankers. One officer who was on parole at Launceston managed to get away with the help of friends in the town and reach Jamaica.

Dartmoor is not the best of places to be on during any winter. In 1813-14 winter a very severe snowstorm cut off Princetown and increased the hardships of the prisoners by food stocks falling perilously low. The snow was 4 feet deep on level ground and with drifting it reached the top of some of the prison buildings. More than 9,000 prisoners and 1,500 soldiers and civilians were dependent for food from Plymouth.

American Prisoners of War

The road was blocked with snow and salt rations had to be issued.

The agent with 200 French prisoners and all the available guards and civilians spent a day in cutting a road to the storehouse where stocks were held. Eventually weather conditions eased and a party were able to make their way down towards Plymouth to obtain emergency supplies. Such was one of the many risks being confined in the midst of the moor.

The United States of America declared war on Great Britain in 1812 through the seizure of boats trying to run the blockade around France. The first draft of 250 American prisoners arrived at Princetown on 3rd April, 1813, who were housed in the already overcrowded French prisoners' quarters. A further 250 were marched up from Plymouth on 28th May, 1813, who were than confined with the *Romans*, a move which would inevitably lead to trouble. However, they settled in tolerably well and before long they were daring enough to manage to make and fly two United States flags on Independence Day from the rooftops. They were ordered to bring the flags down but refused and in the ensuing scuffle one flag was captured but the other hidden by the prisoners.

A clash between the Americans and *Romans* took place on 11th July as soon as the turnkey opened no. 4 prison. The *Romans* lay in wait in the yard armed with stones, knives and clubs then set on the Americans who had strolled over unaware what was ahead of them. Fortunately the outcome was not as bad as could have been; only about forty men were admitted to the infirmary, and prompt action by the guards soon separated the groups and prevented further fighting.

An outbreak of smallpox occurred in August, 1813, which increased the mortality rate tenfold. The epidemic forced the Americans to pull themselves together and, under a change of agent, a better deal was arranged for them so that they could draw on the daily market for any additional goods they wished to purchase.

A further improvement came about through the American government allowing each man 1½d per day for soap and tobacco

as from 1st January, 1814. Immediate social order and decency revived and a body of six was established to regulate the life of the American prisoners. Like the French, the Americans had their own ruffians who caused so much disorder by theiving and fighting that they were separated to two upper floors of no. 4 prison and ruled over by Big Dick, a huge negro who imposed his will on them in no uncertain terms.

Eventually the Americans were given the liberty of all the buildings and market and they then started to copy the pattern of the French prisoners. Some worked at various crafts, others set themselves up selling goods while many went into service with the French officers as waiters.

Following the abdication by Napoleon in April, 1814, the French prisoners started preparing to leave Princetown. They sold to the Americans their tools, etc., and were marched in groups of 500 down to Plymouth. By 20th June the last of the French had left the prison which was given over completely to housing the Americans.

The British government now decided to make Princetown the sole prison for captured Americans and it was not long before drafts of new prisoners started to arrive on the moor. It was not long before they established themselves in a similar manner as the French both socially and industrially. Many were employed on finishing Princetown while others worked as blacksmiths, lamplighters, carpenters, nurses, etc. The conditions of payment for work were the same as the French. This was 6d per day, paid quarterly, and if any man should attempt to escape the whole of the pay of the group would be forfeited and work stopped.

From all accounts the Americans were generally good workers although they had their version of the *Romans*. These were known as *Rough Alleys*, men so despicable in character that they were banished to no. 4 prison to live with the negroes. They revelled in crime and violence and indulged in gambling whenever money came into their hands whether it came from the government daily allowance or by stealing.

In August, 1814, a major plan for a general escape was in hand and all prisoners were sworn to secrecy. The idea was to sink shafts in nos. 4 and 6 buildings twenty feet down and then to tunnel 250 feet to a point beyond the two boundary walls. Work on this grand escape scheme appeared to be progressing without any real difficulties until 60 feet of tunnel was cleared then, without any hint by the guards, they moved in and the idea collapsed. It appears that the tunnels were known to the staff who simply let the work progress to a point where its stoppage would demoralise and put off any further escapes.

Serious trouble broke out in February, 1815, when one prisoner, under sentence of confinement to the cachot, escaped and was hidden in the prison. In spite of strenuous efforts at finding him, he was successful in avoiding detection and, on one occasion, was in hiding under a floor while the building was searched. Under threat of reduced rations and water, the prisoners were still able to hide their man although this defiance almost resulted in a head-on clash between the guards and about 2,000 men when on parade one morning. The prisoner was later found in one of the yards by the turnkey from whom he originally escaped.

The Rebellion of 1814

Hostilities between Great Britain and America ceased with the signing of the Treaty of Ghent of 24th December, 1814. It was quite natural that the prisoners expected to start repatriation at once but because of shipping difficulties this could not be started. By April of the following year there was almost a state of mutiny in the prison which was worsened by shortages of food and bread. Towards the end of the day the *Rough Alley* element forced the gate and made a rush for the storehouse where, to their surprise, bread was being received. This averted trouble for the time.

However, the next day tempers were rising again, this time caused by a guard refusing to return a ball over the wall which had been deliberately kicked out of the yard. The prisoners threatened to climb over if the ball was not returned and when the guard dared them to do this, they started to loosen and break down part of the wall. While this was taking place, the *Rough Alleys* in another section had scaled the picket fence and were skylarking between it and the boundary fence.

As the evening approached a prisoner was reported to have broken the chain securing the main gate watched by a cheering crowd of men. The boundary wall was thought to be broken in five places although, in fact, it had been breached in one place. It was concluded that a mass escape was about to start so the alarm bell was sounded which recalled all the garrison off duty and, also had the effect of bringing out more convicts from their rooms.

The prisoners gathered around the main gate then surged forward into the market area, at the top end, Captain Shortland entered with fifty armed guard. Although it appeared the prisoners were intent on escaping, it was the ruffian element which made the situation much worse than it really was by baiting and jeering the guards. The prisoners were first persuaded to go back inside the gate but pressure from behind forced them forward. A double line of guards now formed across the square and the order was given to charge with fixed bayonets. By now the prisoners were level with the guards which prevented them getting their muskets in position.

In no time at all scuffles broke out and

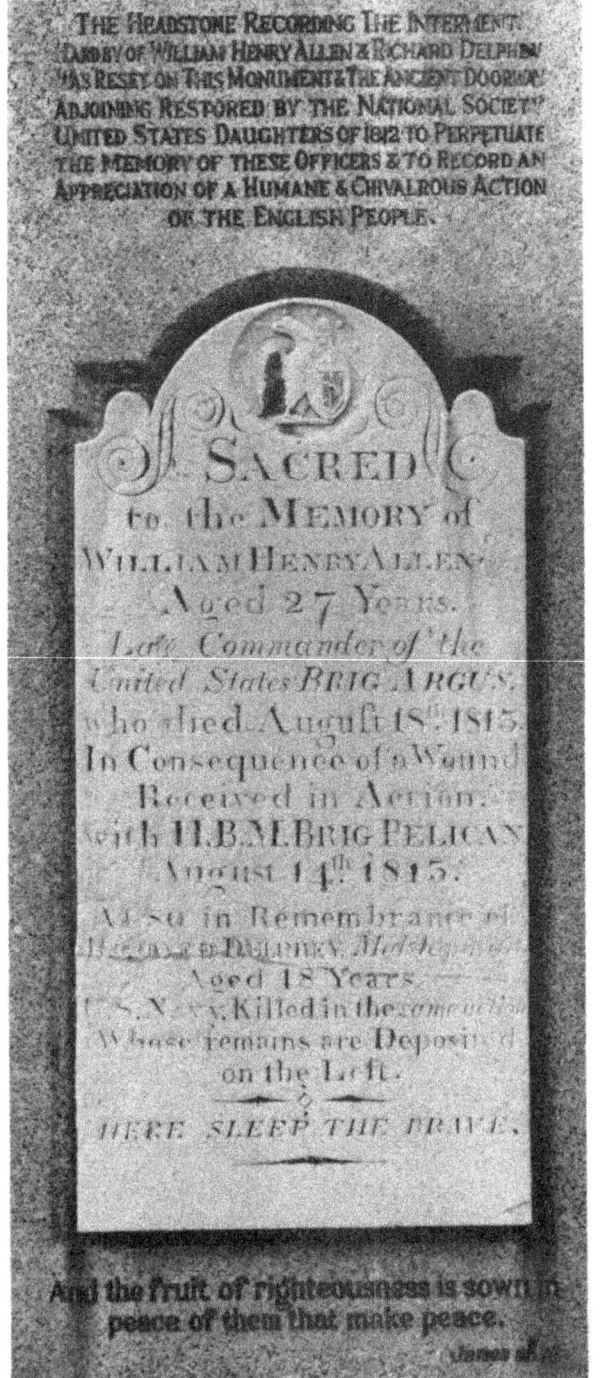

the guards were able to force back some of the prisoners. Stones were thrown at the guards and someone shouted out, 'Fire', whereon the muskets were discharged over the men's heads. This was greeted with jeers and more firing took place, now into the crowd of prisoners and from guards posted around the nearby walls. Confusion reigned for a few minutes with men retreating back into the prison and guards chasing them with fixed bayonets and crossfire coming from the wall.

Although the firing was over in just under three minutes, seven prisoners had been killed and six were so badly wounded that their limbs had to be amputated. Two of these died later. Fifty others had to receive hospital treatment. The government later gave a pension to the wounded and compensation to families who had been bereaved.

The next day a regiment from Plymouth relieved the Somerset Militia, who provided the guards, and in the afternoon an inquiry, under the guidance of the Commander-in-Chief, Plymouth, exonerated Captain Shortland of any personal responsibility. Their report, together with reports from the prisoners, differed so much, that an international inquiry was established to find out whether anyone in particular was to blame for what the Americans called *The Dartmoor Massacre*.

The final outcome was that Captain Shortland was right in thinking that a mass escape was imminent but the subsequent firing was inexcusable.

Commemorative stone, set in the wall of the **Prytsen house Plymouth**, to **Americans** killed in the war in 1812.

Closure of the War Prison

THE days of the old war prison were now fast drawing to a close. On 19th April, 1814, 249 American prisoners were marched down to Plymouth followed a week later by a draft of 350 men. As the hostilities had ceased now for some months, the guards gradually relaxed their control over the prison and men could more or less please themselves whether to stay or escape. The monthly allowance was stopped, the market closed, as there was no money coming into the prison, and the remaining men had to content themselves with the scanty government rations.

A rather ironic situation took place now for many of the French prisoners who had returned to their own country in 1814. Napoleon escaped from Elba, the island prison, landed in France and started to march towards Paris gathering an army of men as he went. This was the start of the 'Hundred Days' war which culminated with his defeat at the Battle of Waterloo on 18th June, 1815.

Many of the former French prisoners found themselves being marched, once again, up from Plymouth to Princetown where they rejoined the remaining 900 American prisoners. These were now all confined in no. 4 building to make room for the return of French prisoners. 4,000 Frenchmen were brought up in the first few days of July and immediately the Americans tried to pass over to them their own possessions, furniture, cooking utensils, etc., as they were expecting to be released at once.

So the prison, once again, heard foreign tongues and saw how the fresh prisoners were beginning to form themselves into groups similar to those of a few years before.

However, this was not to be for very long. The last stay was a very short one as Napoleon surrendered to Captain Maitland on board the *Bellerophon* on 15th July and from 26th July to 8th August he was himself a prisoner a few miles from Princetown on board the boat in Plymouth Sound.

The French prisoners were on the march again and by the 10th February, 1816, the last of the prisoners had left Princetown. The buildings were cleared of stores, the church locked up, and within a few weeks, Princetown took on the appearance of a ghost town with grass growing in the prison yards and nearby streets.

The buildings virtually remained empty from 1816 until 1850 although there were suggestions that they could be used for housing orphans or be used for holding convicts but the cost was too much. So with the passing of the last French prisoners the buildings fell into decay.

The Prison Church

THIS was built by French prisoners of war in 1813 and completed and furnished by the American prisoners in readiness for its first service on 2nd January, 1814. Its rather sombre appearance still reflects the now far off days when Princetown was virtually a community of prisoners and guards, isolated from the rest of Devon.

Although the first period of its use lasted only until 1816, when the church was locked up and kept closed until 1831, this was the time when it served the spiritual needs of the prisoners of war. There are some interesting entries in the records of this period. One reads, *20th May, 1808, Harriet, daughter of Rose Johnson, who was killed in the Trafalgar action, and Elizabeth his wife, born 29th March, 1803*, and another, *19th November, 1815, Catherine Elizabeth, the daughter of Pascal Puchet, serjeant of the 25th Regiment in the service of France, a prisoner at Dartmoor and Hellina Mulder his wife.*

These tell more than what the actual words say about just two families caught up in the upsurge of war and the effect it has on people of different nations. It does not take much thought to imagine this church during these early years when services were conducted in French and English coloured with a strong Devonshire dialect.

St. Michael's and All Angels is built of Dartmoor granite with a high tower which can be seen for many miles around. The interior is a little plain and there is a Jacobean pulpit which came from a church in Exeter. Almost all the memorials and flags say something about the link between the church and prison and to those who are buried here.

Following the opening of the prison for convicts in 1850, the church assumed a different role and another story emerges from its records. The first convict to be buried here was William Tegg, aged 33 years, who died on 31st May, 1851, the first of dozens over the years whose graves remained unmarked until 1902. At one period there was an average of three burials a day which seems exceptionally high for any institution confining adults under what must have been harsh conditions.

The building has been restored from time to time. Once after the interior was gutted by fire in 1868, another time in 1897, and again a few years later when the east wall was in danger of collapsing.

The east window was unveiled in 1910 as a memorial to the 218 American prisoners who died in the prison.

The Criminal Prison 1850

WHY was the old war prison converted to use as a criminal prison having stood for many years empty and neglected? Up until the 1840's, criminals were either executed or transported to the Colonies, Australia or, last of all, Tasmania. This practice could not go on for ever as these countries refused to accept any more criminals and, in any case, Tasmania was simply getting full up with them.

The government were forced to requisition buildings for housing men convicted and decided in 1849 that Dartmoor could be put to use for this need. So it was that the prison took on its second and major role for confining men for criminal offences.

In September, 1850, no. 3 prison was made fit for occupation and quarters were prepared for warders and military guard. On the 2nd November, 1850, the first draft of prisoners, 95 men, were marched up to the moor to become the first of hundreds to spend part of their life within its granite walls. Captain Gambier, the first governor, arrived on the 4th with another 95 prisoners. The staff comprised of 24 with the assistance of 80 military personnel.

By the end of the year buildings had been fitted up to receive 1,300 convicts and two were opened up for use as sick bays where hammocks were strung to hold some 700 men. Parts of the old buildings were converted into the bakehouse, kitchen and chapel.

It was not long before the staff were faced with troubles of one kind or another, first from escape attempts, even within weeks of the prison opening, and minor disturbances and attacks on warders.

A mutiny occurred in no. 2 prison in January, 1852, but the ringleader was caught and placed in solitary confinement. It was found out the next day that he had tried to cut his way out with the iron heel of his boot. Since then men confined in punishment cells wear slippers, not their working boots. On 8th November of the same year one prisoner managed to hide himself in the gashouse chimney from which he made his escape to freedom two days later and was never caught.

A very severe blizzard swept over the moor in February, 1853, meat wagons were snowed up at Merrivale and the prisoners placed on half rations. Water and gas supplies failed and the general situation for all the inhabitants at Princetown looked very bleak.

Notable Events

A party of 100 convicts was mustered to cut a path down to the meat wagons, three warders set out with spades to try to get through to Tavistock with the mail while two privates of the military guard foolishly set out from Dousland to try to reach Princetown. Another guard went out to try to find them but none were found until the next morning when all three were located in a drift at Peak Hill frozen to death. A tablet records this event in the church.

Hardly a year went by at Princetown without some trouble either from the weather or from the discontent of the prisoners. On 15th March, 1854, a mutiny broke out and four warders were attacked. A little later the deputy governor was assaulted as he was leaving the chapel and a similar fate befell the chaplain. Such was part of the risks staff took trying to contain 1,000 or more men convicted of criminal offences. On another occasion a warder was cut down with a spade and an assistant stabbed.

Assaults on warders became so serious that cases were brought up at the Exeter Assizes and heavy sentences meted out in an endeavour to try to reduce the attacks. Also the military guard was replaced by a civilian guard but both measures had little effect in curbing the disturbances.

In the 1860's the weak-minded prisoners were transferred to another prison and juveniles sent in their place. These were young boys who turned out to be just as difficult as the other prisoners as the following year a plot came to light in which they planned to attack a warder with knives.

The records, once again, tell of recurring severe winters and one reads that a prison schoolmaster was found frozen to death having tried to get back from Tavistock during a storm. The snow was five feet deep on the level and again parties of convicts were formed to try to dig a path to the meat carts and clear the leat of ice. Conditions during the winter must have been very harsh in the prison as there was no heating during the early years.

The summer months saw many of the prisoners working on the moor, on the prison buildings, cutting peat and tending the gardens. The peat cutting was particularly disliked by the convicts and one man bluntly refused to do this work. Upon being taken to the governor he displayed his hatred by throwing his boots at him.

Criminal prisoners were not the only kind confined to Dartmoor. In the 1870's members of the Fenians, a secret society made up of

Irish and Irish-Americans, were sent to the moor. A series of explosions to public buildings occurred and an attempt was foiled to blow up Clerkenwell prison to free members of this society. One of the men sentenced to death for his part in these attacks was the last person to be hanged publicly in this country. A change in the law only permitted hangings to take place in prisons after this time.

Improvements to conditions and prisoners' welfare continued to take place from time to time, especially after outbreaks of serious trouble which were often exaggerated by the newspapers. A commission on penal servitude was conducted under Lord Kimberley, the outcome of which was that prisoners were allowed to petition the Home Secretary and visitors were appointed to inspect the prison periodically.

An unusual occurance took place in 1890 when an ex-convict negro was found breaking into the prison. He had been discharged a month previously and vowed that he would get his own back on the chief warder. He had walked from London and managed to get into the prison area where he was found. He was later tried at Tavistock for burglary and said that it was his intention to set fire to the prison.

By the turn of the century the conditions and running of the prison had changed considerably from the 1850's. In 1903 the Prince and Princess of Wales visited Princetown and during the Great War many convicts were released for service in the army. During the hostilities the prison held many conscientious objectors and it was not until 1919 that convicts were being confined here.

There was no letting up in escape attempts, some of which are listed on the cover of this booklet. They are almost too numerous to list. Despite all the security precautions, patrols and regular checks, they are still occurring from time to time. No doubt with such a large number of men confined within the boundary walls, there is bound to be some successful escapes.

These two photographs show prisoners working at the turn of the century in the quarry and gathering mangold wurzels from the prison farm. The scenes differ considerably from to-day by the change in uniform, the close supervision and the less harsh conditions prevailing at Princetown. Both the quarry and the farm methods of working have been extensively modernised and compare very favourably with similar commercial enterprises.

N.B. Mangold wurzels are a large form of beet which is used as cattle feed.

The 1932 Mutiny

THIS was a black year for the prison when almost all the inmates rioted and set fire or damaged the buildings causing some £3,000 worth of damage. Forty-one convicts were hurt and twenty-four staff suffered various injuries.

The mutiny broke out on Sunday morning, 24th January, 1932, soon getting out of hand with looting and burning. The old administrative block, containing the Governor's office and records, was set alight, the bell tower and escape bell came crashing down and the windows of the officers' mess and chapels smashed in. Cells were unlocked to release prisoners and furnishings damaged.

It soon became apparent that some strong measures had to be taken to first control and then break up the rioting. This was accomplished when a detachment of county police was called in and a baton charge made which resulted in the majority of the injuries occurring, although others came about by some prisoners beating up one another.

The medical staff were able to move freely among the prisoners and staff tending to wounds and some of the inmates actually gave protection to the staff when they were cornered.

On Monday a detachment of the 2nd Battalion of the Worcester Regiment stood guard around the prison but was with drawn a day or so later. A special Assize Court was set up at Princetown at which thirty convict leaders were charged with riotous behaviour. Various punishments were given out ranging from twelve years to a few months after which the prisoners were sent to other prisons. Commendations were made to other prisoners for assistance during the rioting and existing sentences were reduced.

The Prison To-day

THE running of the modern prison today bears little resemblance to the former war prison or even to the first fifty years or so when it was opened as a criminal prison. The buildings do, however, retain more than a flavour of the Victorian years and the general layout of them are still based on the plan of the war prison. The entrance area, if any, retains more atmosphere of the old days than the other areas of the prison.

There is, in fact, a surprising number of modern or adapted buildings and huts which now serve specialist purposes outside the actual need for confining men in the cell blocks. Accommodation for staff and prison officers can be seen near the prison and more land has been taken up with farming and similar activities.

The kind of person confined here has also changed considerably and the numbers reduced to around 500 with a staff of about 250 which includes visitors and instructors

in the various workshops. The majority of the prisoners are recidivists, that is those who have served at least one previous sentence and spend between 3 and 10 years here according to the scale of their offence. Many of the men are treated as 'trusties' and are allowed certain privileges of access to areas of the prison otherwise barred and can engage in work activities without direct supervision. For example, the small weather-recording unit from which information is sent about conditions on the moor, is maintained by one of these inmates.

The daily routine is laid down as follows which allows much more free time than many realise:

0630 hours	Reveille
0700 ,,	Breakfast
0815 ,,	Tally, exercise and work
1200 ,,	Dinner
1345 ,,	Tally, exercise and work
1645 ,,	Tea
1830–1930 hours	Evening Classes
1930–2100 ,,	Evening Association
2230 hours	Lights out

A wide variety of activities and pursuits can be engaged in by the inmates who wish to gain knowledge about subjects or acquire skill and training in trades for possible use when they are released. The prison is served by many visiting lecturers and courses take place on a wide variety of subjects. One inmate was reported to have gained a degree through correspondence work here and, following release, was admitted to a college for further advancement.

The evening association period is one set aside for privileged men to participate in various group activities. Recreational facilities for these includes watching TV programmes,

ments to take place here is the training available in different skills and trades. Gone are the days of the treadwheel and picking oakum. Now the scene is one of well-equipped workshops, operating with trained civilian instructors, in blacksmith work, carpentry, general metal work and even a television assembly shop linked to a Devon company on a production basis. Tailoring and shoe repair work and almost all the maintenance work on the buildings can be also done. These activities form part of the rehabilitation programme for men which gives them confidence, first in themselves, and in holding down a job in the outside world. Inmates are also employed in assisting as mates to officer tradesmen in plumbing, bricklaying, painting and decorating and in electrical work.

A surprising feature of the prison complex is the extent of the development and progress

table tennis, darts, snooker and billiards and a record player in each main block.

Prisoners are allowed one visit from relatives or friends every four weeks but no more than three persons can see any inmate at once. The medical facilities and trained staff can normally tackle any emergency cases that may arise without need to take prisoners to hospital. There is a well-equipped minor operating theatre, dental room and a sick bay where a host of minor complaints can be dealt with quickly and efficiently. An X-ray unit and developing facilities can adequately cope with the normal bone fractures and breakages that occur from time to time.

Perhaps one of the most beneficial develop-

made in running a hill farm. There are about 1,600 acres of land given over to this which employs many men in a variety of husbandry duties. The farm is stocked with a dairy herd of cattle, a beef herd of about 350 head, some store pigs and about 500 sheep. The progeny of these animals is fattened and sold in the local towns. Market gardening is extensively engaged in for supplying produce to the prison and even aforestation enables training to take place and offer a ready supply of timber to the prison. It is these features that often surprise the visitor to Princetown more than the actual view of the prison buildings. Many of the activities make this prison almost independent of outside resources in running from day to day.

There are good cooking and kitchen facilities and, once again, men can be engaged and trained in preparing food under instructors and be encouraged to consider taking up this kind of work after discharge. The same situation applies to the large laundry which caters for the cleaning needs of the inmates, hospital and workshops.

The site of one of the old blocks is now covered with a large gymnasium which is equipped for as many physical exercises as one can imagine. These take place under trained supervision and guidance and range from game sports to individual physical education exercises with balls, ropes, bars and weights. Football matches are extremely popular between groups of inmates and are always being played when weather permits in the games area. Team activities encourage men to be more responsive to one another and help towards redirecting inmates to lead a better life after serving their sentences.

Arts and crafts activities often appear in the local newspapers especially when exhibitions of work were staged in the prison and the public allowed to view them. A considerable amount of time, talent and ingenuity goes into making furnishings, toys, paintings, dolls houses, etc. If there is a link between the prison of today and the prison of yesterday, it is this expression of creativeness on the part of some men to make things of a very high standard. The modern counterpart of the boneships is the fine wood and metalwork produced in the workshops.

Other aspects of this institution include a well-furnished inter-denominational chapel, personal visits to men by trained and voluntary social workers and a general atmosphere of encouragement to make the inmate take pride in himself and in his ability at fitting in with society after he leaves the moor.

Security

Security is, of course, uppermost in the minds of the prison authorities whose constant vigilance has prevented many escapes while the moor itself has proved an ally in adding another barrier to the would be escapee. The most apparent obstacle seen by the visitor for maintaining security is the wall although there are a variety of procedures which are followed but not so evident. These included the pony patrols, for around the prison area, and the dog patrols for the prison grounds. Regular searches are carried out and spot checks made throughout the buildings. Security is the first responsibility of every officer whatever job or activity he may be doing. The pony patrols are now no longer used.

A view of one of the many cells arranged in blocks on different floors which face the centre of each building. The neat and plain furnishings, with books, make the cell reasonable living quarters for the inmates.

Produce from the greenhouse helps towards feeding in the prison. Flowers are also grown and training given to men in general gardening work under the guidance of experienced staff.

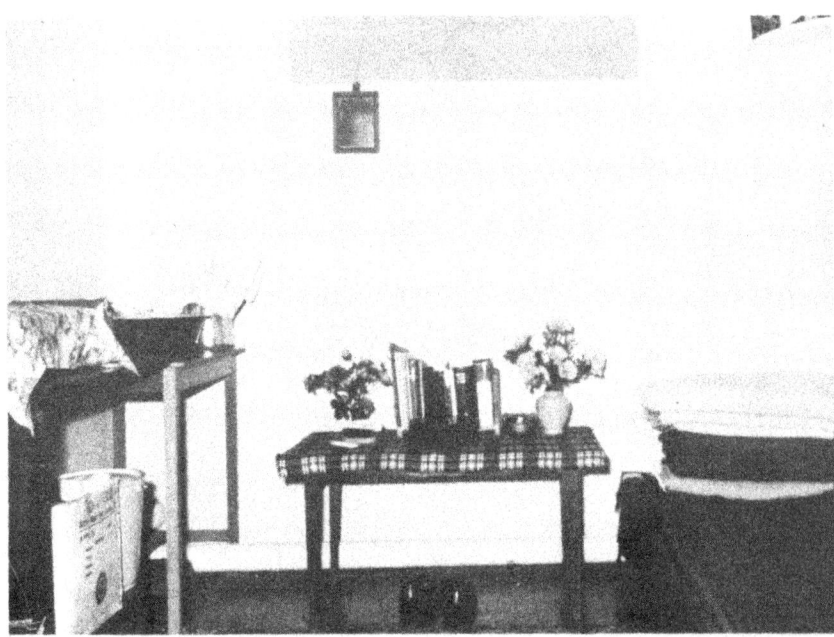

Work in the Prison

A surprising range of work is produced at Dartmoor from small decorative metal work to heavy iron products for use in the prison. The workshops are equipped with modern machines and men have the opportunity of gaining skills under expert supervision or of undertaking creative work for interest and pleasure. Some of this kind of work is often included in the exhibitions staged of the inmates' craft activities. These illustrations show two aspects of this, one of the link with industry in the area handling components of television sets, and the other of producing decorative metalwork. Training for work after leaving the prison is part of the policy of rehabilitating men and making Dartmoor as self-reliant as possible.

Recreational Activities

Two aspects of the prison's recreational activities are seen here which the inmates are encouraged to use. The large gymnasium provides opportunities for many games and a variety of physical education exercises that can help to develop new interests and get men involved in group games. Instruction is given by trained staff and individual help given to men who wish to pursue a greater interest in physical recreation.

The prison library is well stocked with over 10,000 titles ranging from light novels to text books for educational purposes. It is managed by a prison officer and also handles the newspapers and magazines which can be bought by the inmates. Provision is also made for men who have reading and writing difficulties through direct tuition and correspondence work.

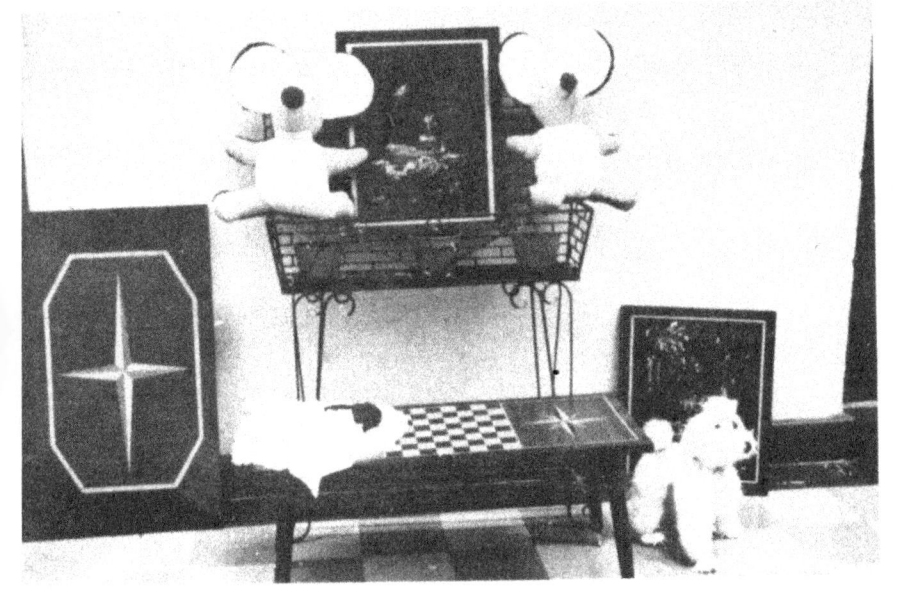

Some of the many varied items made by the inmates can be seen in this photograph which have formed part of an exhibition of their work. A very high standard of proficiency and imaginative skill is reached by men working during their recreational periods.

Men relaxing playing a game of snooker in one of the prison buildings. This is allowed during the evening association period.

On the homeward journey: one of the jobs is to ensue that men who are about to leave are well kitted out with clothes. The reception and discharge unit also keeps in safe custody clothing and effects of men during their time at Princetown.

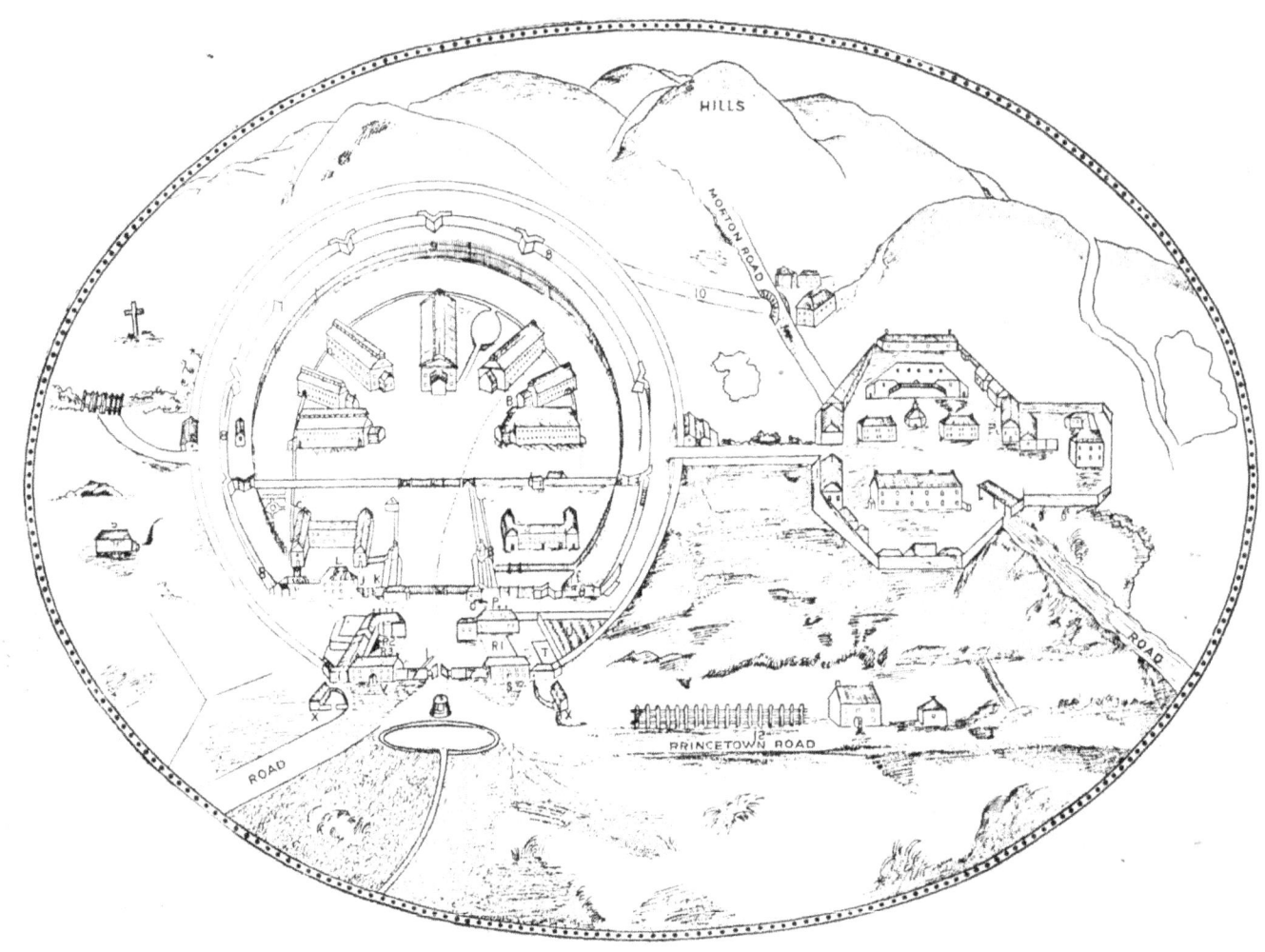

PLAN OF THE WAR PRISON, 1809 to 1816

SOLDIERS IMPRISONED AT DARTMOOR

French Imperial Guard Grenadiers: White trousers and long white boots. Blue tailed jacket with red epaulets. Red cockade worn above busby type headgear.

Imperial Guard Dragoons: White trousers, long black boots. White waistcoat over green jacket. Long red cockade worn above highly decorated helmet, with long black tail hanging from rear of helmet.

French Imperial Guard Engineers: Blue tight fitting uniform, long white boots. Red epaulets, cockaded helmet with long curved black plume from back to front.

American New York Rifle Corps: Green loose fitting uniform, trimmed with yellow, jacket and trousers. Side hat also green with green cockade.

American 16th Infantry Regiment: Long tight fitting trousers. White waistcoat, black tunic. Red and white collar and cuffs. Tall peaked cap, black. Silver plume in front.

Arthur L. Clamp – the man behind the books

Arthur Leslie Clamp was a man of boundless energy with a passion for helping others, particularly through his love of history. A printer by trade, he started his career in a printing company before moving his family from Exeter to Plymouth to teach at the Plymouth College of Art and Design, where he eventually became the Head of the Printing Department.

A Devoted Family Man

Despite his love of teaching, Arthur prioritised his family, always making it home by 5:30pm for tea. He and his wife, Rosemary, raised five children: Susan, Angela, Elizabeth, David, and Steven. Arthur would often combine his love of family and history by taking his children on Sunday walks, encouraging them to appreciate historical monuments by taking photos or making crayon rubbings of gravestones for his books. The family home at 203 Elburton Road was a hub of activity, with a large garden, featuring a two-storey fort and a makeshift swimming pool.

Arthur with his five children.

A Lifelong Learner and Adventurer

Arthur's thirst for knowledge extended beyond history to a deep curiosity about the world. He was passionate about exploring different cultures, traditions, and cuisines, often taking advantage of his long summer holidays as a teacher to travel to places like India, Russia, South America, the middle east and the USA, sometimes bringing one of his children along. This adventurous spirit even influenced his home life, as seen by the short-lived family tradition of steam-cooking vegetables after a trip to Iceland.

History is a prominent feature of family days out

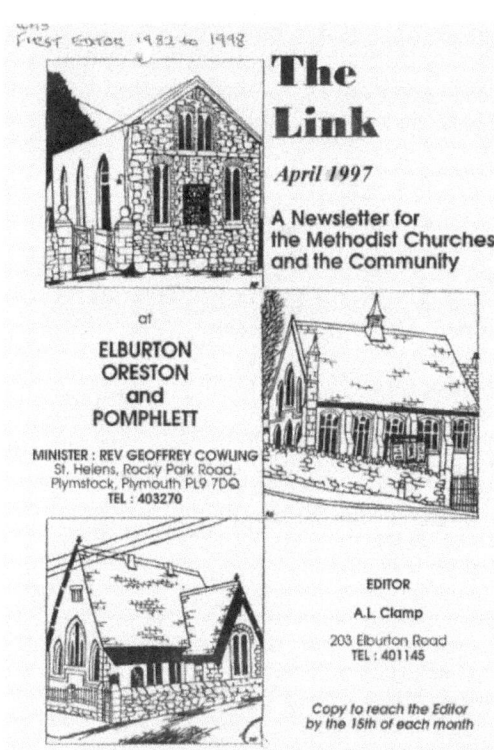

Community and Philanthropic Spirit

His commitment to serving others was evident in his long-standing involvement with the Elburton Methodist Church. He was the Sunday School Superintendent for over 15 years and served as the editor of the wider church's monthly newsletter, "The Link," for a similar duration. After Rosemary's very sad passing, Arthur later remarried and, following a chance encounter with a professor from India, established a connection with a missionary school in Chennai. Together with his new wife, Christine, he co-founded a "Sponsor a Child's Education" program that continues to this day.

Pictured left – The cover of 'The Link' complete with hand drawn sketches of each church by Angela
Below right – Arthur Clamp promoting his latest book
Below left – Arthur at home with his first wife, Rosemary
Below centre – Arthur on holiday with his second wife, Christine

A Legacy of Learning and Positivity

Arthur's greatest passion was history, which he brought to life through tireless research, documentation, and the many books he authored. He was driven by a need to "never be stuck in a rut," constantly seeking new experiences, meeting new people, and expanding his knowledge. With a positive attitude and a great sense of humour, he was always ready to help others, leaving a lasting impact on his family and community. His children, Susan, Angela, Elizabeth, David, and Steven, remember him with love and gratitude.

David Clamp, 2025

A Legacy of Local History

Below is the story of how Arthur L Clamp began writing books, in his own words, drafted shortly before he passed away in 2001. I have only made minor alterations to this text, correcting grammatical errors that he did not survive to correct himself. When I first discovered this text, I was shocked to see my name mentioned. It seems that, unbeknownst to me, I shared my first PC with him. I suspect he used it during the day when I was at school, although I do have one memory of sitting with him and showing him how it worked. It has been a pleasure to pick up where he left off and see his books republished and redistributed, and to know that I was part of the story, even back then. It was also fascinating to discover that his pricing structure matches the way I have tried to price the books, with a third going to local sellers and the rest covering printing costs with a little left over for my expenses.

I am his eldest grandson, and it is a privilege to curate his legacy, which we are calling 'The Clamp Collection'. The very last line of the text originally reads "The following pages list all the titles." Sadly, that page is missing and we have no record of all the books he published and knowing that some of those were researched by other authors makes the process of finding them even harder. I look forward to one day completing the collection and seeing them all available again. And maybe, one day, I'll even start writing my own to add to the series. For now, here is his story in his own words.

Steven Gibson, 2025

Writing and Publishing Booklets on Local Topics and Areas

I started this interest in either 1968 or 1969 when living in Woodford. I had by these dates established the Department of Printing and I think I must have been looking for something different to do. The first titles were of A5 size proofed from type set at Clarke, Doble and Brendon, Ltd., Plymouth printers, and then made up into pages and printed at Sawtell and Neilson, Ltd., Totnes.

Then began a slow process of getting them out to shops, etc. which proved to be more time consuming and difficult than actually researching, writing and getting the books into print. However, I persisted and opened a business account with Barclays Bank on the Broadway. I was advised to give it a title so I called it "Westway Publications". There came along another problem, one of storage of paper and finished books which was solved when the family moved to Elburton in 1970.

I changed the printer to Penwell, Ltd., Callington, Cornwall, as he was then just setting up himself and his prices seemed very reasonable. I did not get any of the printers to make up the complete books. I hand folded the flat printed sheets, stitched the books on a small manual table stitcher and trimmed them in a small hand turned guillotine which I bought from someone in Penzance for £40. It was brought up in a van.

The trouble and time going to and fro to Callington was too much so I transferred the printing to PDS Printers, Prince Rock, Plymouth, and I have been with them ever since. Now they are at Plympton which is easy to reach and they fold the flat sheets which was turning out to be a long chore which only saved a small part of the printing costs.

All my first titles were written by myself. I took the photographs and developed them in the loft of the house, the type was set by now on a computer situated in the house at Elburton from which I had collected photographic lengths of text to cut up and law down as pages.

At some point I decided that I would do my own film processing of lith film so I bought a large second hand process camera from Kingsbridge and learnt through trial and error to make line negatives of the text and halftone negatives of the illustrations which proved more difficult than I anticipated. The main problem was trying to keep the developer in the large dish at the correct temperature as any change would affect the developing time. I replaced this old camera with a brand new one bought from Croydon, Surrey, costing £900. This has turned out to be a great asset cutting out an expensive part of the printer's costs and one crucial aspect of the work which I could control.

By the middle 1970s there were many outlets I had contacted in Plymouth, up to Dartmoor, Exeter, around to Torbay, Totnes, Dartmouth and the South Hams. The market for local books was much greater than I had first thought and through getting to know many local people undertaking research themselves had the chance to help and make up books for other people who had in most instances, got together a collection of photographs with some text in a rather muddled way. Through my experience in print I was able to shape up their work and get it into print and in every case I had to pay the printer and let the person have the royalties. In the majority of titles produced in this manner this was another way of producing titles and it did give some profit to my work. However, I must say that in a few cases I lost out by either the other person getting the numbers wrong, not returning any monies from stock I delivered or they thought that more of their books should have been sold.

The print run was usually 1,000 copies and from time to time I have had reprints of 250 copies. It took about ten years to clear the first print run so I always had large stocks in the garage, workshop, etc. The numbers sold during the early years was about 7,000 copies a year increasing to around 9,000 copies and for the whole of the enterprise about 500,000 have been sold. The booklets have become part of the local scene and many people collect them, shops regularly order copies and I go around certain areas month by month restocking or replacing titles as necessary.

During the past year or so I have started setting the text on a Packard Bell PC, something which I should have done some years back. I share it with Steven Gibson, my grandson. There appears to be no end to the market for local books, but I could not earn a regular income because of the long time it takes to sell stock.

However, now exceeding 100 titles made up mainly of A4 twenty-four page booklets, some folded guides, with selling prices set with a third going to the shop which is the trade custom, the original idea has been quite successful and could go on for ever.

Apart from monetary benefits, however spasmodically these might be, I have learnt a lot myself, met many interesting people and have become part of the local scene with requests to give talks and to advise people about getting into print.

Arthur L Clamp, 2001

Death of local historical author

'He was an incredible character who was just loved by everybody who knew him'

A WELL-loved Elburton author has died at the age of 68.

Arthur Clamp (pictured right), who was one of the West Country's most successful writers, died at St Luke's Hospice, Turnchapel, after losing his battle against cancer.

Tributes have been flooding in for a man who was known in the community as a prominent writer and outgoing person.

He produced more than 140 titles during his life, dealing with both fiction, fact and history, often discussing West Country topics that were close to his heart.

One of his most acclaimed books was *The Plymouth Blitz* and he also won credit for *The Rise and Fall of the Bearings of Membland Hall*, set in Noss Mayo.

He achieved sales of between 7,000 and 9,000 books every year and it is estimated that he has sold over half a million books, covering the areas of Plymouth, Dartmoor, Exeter, Torbay and the South Hams.

Mr Clamp was born in Mitcham, Surrey, in 1932, and was the eldest of four children.

He moved to Devon in 1941 to avoid the London air-raids.

Mr Clamp trained as a printer in Exeter and also gained a teachers' certificate in 1959 from Garnet College in London.

Plymouth College of Art, however, was to prove to be Mr Clamp's working home for the following 32 years until 1991, when he retired as head of the printing department.

He had a great interest in travel and had visited the USA, Tanzania, China, Russia, Peru, as well as travelling across Europe, where he presented talks and slide shows on his experiences as a writer.

Mr Clamp was a member of Elburton Methodist Church for many years, superintendent of the Sunday school and editor of the church newsletter, as well as being involved in much charity work.

He was president of the Plymouth and District Field Club and an active member of the Elburton Residents' Association.

He enjoyed leading walks on Dartmoor and historical tours throughout the West Country.

Mr Clamp married his first wife, Rosemary, in 1956 and they had five children – Susan, Angela, Elizabeth, David and Steven – and she died in 1987. He also had 11 grandchildren.

He leaves a wife Christine, after remarrying in 1991, and her two children and three grandchildren.

'He was an incredible character who was just loved by everybody who knew him,' said his wife.

'He will be missed by his family, his friends, the people he worked with and just everybody who knew him through his books.'

More than 300 mourners attended his funeral at Elburton Methodist Church on Monday.

The attendance was a celebration of his life – he would have found that really special. It shows his vibrancy and love of people,' said Mrs Clamp.

Steven Clamp added that his father was 'a well respected and loved man, missed by a great many people throughout the South West and far beyond'.

Picture contributed

This newspaper article, published by the Evening Herald on 17th August 2001, forms a good record of his life. Just as he encourages us to learn more about local history, we encourage you to learn a little about him. For that reason, we have included these pages at the back of all the most recently republished books, in honour of his memory and recognition of his contribution to the community.

www.ingramcontent.com/pod-product-compliance
Lightning Source LLC
Chambersburg PA
CBHW061405070526
44584CB00031B/4170